Deconstructing Church:
The Allure of The Machine and The Hope for a Better Way

ANTHONY ANDERSON

Copyright © 2015 Anthony Anderson

All rights reserved.

ISBN: 152371266X
ISBN-13: 978-1523712663

Unless otherwise indicated, all Scripture quotations are taken from the Holy Bible, New Living Translation, copyright © 1996, 2004, 2007, 2013 by Tyndale House Foundation. Used by permission of Tyndale House Publishers, Inc., Carol Stream, Illinois 60188. All rights reserved.

Scripture quotations marked (NIV) are taken from the Holy Bible, New International Version®, NIV®. Copyright © 1973, 1978, 1984, 2011 by Biblica, Inc.™ Used by permission of Zondervan. All rights reserved worldwide. www.zondervan.com The "NIV" and "New International Version" are trademarks registered in the United States Patent and Trademark Office by Biblica, Inc.™

Scripture quotations marked (ESV) are from The Holy Bible, English Standard Version® (ESV®), copyright © 2001 by Crossway, a publishing ministry of Good News Publishers. Used by permission. All rights reserved.

Edited by Maria Isabel Sanchez Delgado
Cover Art by Joshua Nicholson

DEDICATION

To Emily, who stood by me all these years. And to my children, whose antics will continue to provide anecdotes for decades. I love you.

CONTENTS

THE INVITATION — 1

THE PREMISE — 3

THE DILEMMAS — 5

Dilemma 1: Are We Building an Organization or Disciplers? — 7

Dilemma 2: Are We Seeing Church Needs or Seeing Individuals? — 15

Dilemma 3: Are We Telling People What They Should Do or Inviting Them Into What We Are Doing? — 21

Dilemma 4: Are We Letting Big Church Inform Everyday Life or Everyday Life Inform Big Church? — 29

THE ALTERNATIVE — 37

The Alternative — 39

The Church Should Be Going — 43

The Church Should Be Loving — 45

The Church Should Be Equipping — 47

The Church Should Be Encouraging — 49

The Church Should Be Empowering — 51

The Church Should Be Confessing — 55

The Church Should Be A Body — 57

The Church Should Be A Family — 61

THE DREAM — 65

Appendix — 73

THE INVITATION

Imagine that you've been approached on the street with a once-in-a-lifetime opportunity. The offer seems completely legitimate, and there's no disclaimer or fine-print involved. They are looking for a group of average, everyday people to travel to an automobile manufacturing plant and watch as an entire car is disassembled, piece by piece. They assure you that you will be explained the details of each part along the way so that you have a much better working knowledge of the vehicle. And at the end, you will be given an opportunity to reassemble the car, together with everyone else participating. The challenge? To build a working vehicle that uses only the necessary parts in order to have a more efficient, more economical, and overall better experience when driving. In essence, they will pull back the curtain on car manufacturing and then allow you the chance to design your own car, armed with your newfound insight.

This is admittedly a dangerous proposition. The average person has very little understanding of cars, other than how to turn one on, operate it, and refill the gas tank. But the same is not true with Christians in regard to the church.

Many of us grew up in the church. Many of us have spent hours poring over the scripture. We have devoted time in prayer, in bible studies, and attending weekly services. We have inklings of how the church is supposed to work. We know perhaps more than we would give ourselves credit for.

What most of us don't know is what goes on behind the curtain. We haven't seen the decisions that lead to the processes and programs that our church implements. We go along with what is presented because we have a blind faith that our church leadership has our best interests at heart. And, most of the time, they do.

But have you ever wanted to peek in for just a moment? Has your curiosity become aroused from time to time as you wondered what led to the current decisions being made?

This book is an attempt at doing just that. As such, we take a look at three important areas. The first section, The Dilemmas are technical, snappy, and fact-driven. They do their best to peel back the curtain of decades of ministry and church leadership to show the rest of us what goes on behind the scenes and what drives those decisions.

Next, The Alternative looks at scripture and identifies key components that are mandated to be a part of every church body. It contains a number of passages and digs in deep to understand what Jesus was calling us to do and to become.

And finally, The Dream offers a ray of hope. It provides a possible avenue of pursuit for each of us, whether we work in church leadership, Christian ministry, or are simply normal, everyday people in the workplace. It is a direction in which we might run in order to better follow our Lord and Savior and away from the machine that we've built.

So, what do you say? It's an invitation of a lifetime. Would you like to come watch a church be disassembled? And even more importantly, would you like to be a part of putting it back together-better than ever?

THE PREMISE

There is an epidemic in today's church that looks to be squarely the fault of the everyday believer. What's the problem? Lack of interest and participation in the more "advanced" programs and activities taking place within the church—the things expected of longtime believers who have moved beyond simply showing up on Sundays. The Purpose Driven Church model would say that people are having trouble rounding first (membership) and heading to second base (discipleship). Missional-minded folks would say that believers have become merely consumers instead of producers.

What they're really all saying is that it's extremely hard to get people to show up to small groups, actively serve, and grow in any meaningful way outside of the Sunday gathering. Typical believers show up for an hour a week to get their fix and head off to their other lives with little more than an afterthought of the two worlds colliding. The reaction from churches is to make more prominent their need for volunteers, offer more service projects, and dumb down the "requirements" to lead a group, teach a class, or run Sunday School. We broadcast the message from the pulpit that those in the pews should more actively "be the church," "get out and do something," and "stop being consumers," all the while striving to make a dent in the spiritual development of each attendee in the 30 short minutes they have to communicate with them.

The only real development from this entire mess is that the church leadership grows continually disheartened by the seeming lack of interest and passion from its attendees; the believers grow disgruntled at constantly being berated while not feeling like there is an adequate alternative, and the entire entity that is the church continues to grind to a near halt. Yes, there will always be glimpses of hope, pockets of growth, and outliers who just "get it."

Unfortunately though, in large part, the reason churches are so desperate to grow is not so much that they are able to better impact their city, but in the hope that they might able to *finally begin* to impact their city.

This tension is real. We feel it in the way we interact with each other on Sundays. We hear it in the frustrated pleas from the stage. We see it in the eyes of the people we grab lunch with after the gathering. If this is what our souls are longing for, why does it feel more like a chore list than the priorities of the Spirit's desires? If this is what we're supposed to be doing, why does it feel so joyless?

What if there was a better way? What if we looked to the scripture to find our mandates rather than seeking popular business models for our answers? What if the simple answer was that the more we get bigger, the more we should be getting smaller?

I've been involved in church ministry my entire life. As a pastor's kid, I guess I was born into it. My first real foray into leadership of any kind began sixteen years ago, and I've been involved in full-time ministry for very nearly a decade now. I'm not telling you any of this to convince you that I'm any sort of expert or that my large body of experience has given me a solution to all of our problems as a church. I'm actually trying to do the opposite.

This isn't the first book ever written on the subject, and it certainly won't be the last. So, when you read this book, I hope you approach it with the same amount of humble desperation that I am as I write to you. Not that we have proudly attained any secret knowledge, but that we have wallowed in the mire of mediocrity and complacency long enough and are looking for a way out through the lens of divine discontent.

We will take a look at four dilemmas faced by (and frankly, created by) the modern church and then peer down a rabbit hole that might just provide a way out of the muck that many of us are feeling we've fallen into. And as we progress, I hope we can establish a firm scriptural foundation for what may not be "the way," but is certainly an admirable pursuit of The Way.

THE DILEMMAS

Dilemma 1: Are We Building an Organization or Disciplers?

The first problem with our current model lies in the fact that we have built an untamable, uncontrollable "big church" system that demands so much time, energy, and manpower that it requires all hands on deck to maintain. And the larger the congregation grows, the more people we need to help check the rigging, grab an oar, start bailing out water, or any other number of cheesy sailing analogies. And so we spend our time slotting people into a job in the big crew when perhaps what we should be doing is training them how to navigate the seas and helping them build their own ship and crew.

What I'm trying to say is that the problem with big church is that its direct and indirect focus inevitably is itself. Self-maintenance and even self-preservation gets the majority of our time, and we're left with only small bits of time to beg people to go out and do something—to be something—more than what we've taken the time to train them for. Unfortunately, that's the way it works. The bigger the machine gets, the more we begin to rely on the machine to do the work for us, and our time is spent on keeping the machine working rather than doing the work that the machine is now doing for us.

Anyone who owns a car, computer, or smartphone knows this to be true. The more advanced our technologies and toys become, the less time we spend doing the work and the more time we spend looking for ways to fix our devices, upgrade them, or trade them in for better, newer models. The business and manufacturing world is experiencing this as well. While many are worried that at our current pace robotics and automation will replace many factory and service jobs and render even more hard-working humans unemployed, the truth of the matter is that for every person replaced on the factory line, there's a job opening to design and another to service the very machine that's taking jobs away. And while that slide in emphasis may work in manufacturing where a personal, human touch doesn't always make that much of a difference, apply the same model to the church—a place where personal, human interaction is an absolute necessity—well, you can see where the system begins to fall apart. We would like for you to engage with your co-workers after hours about the truth of the gospel of Jesus, but what we would love even more is that you bolt early every Thursday night so you're not late to worship practice. We want you to invite your neighbors over for dinner and experience true community, but what's even more important is that you make sure to invite them to church on Sunday.

So where did we start to drift? Like in most things, I believe the major fault lies in our constant need to paint our worlds in black and white. In some way, I'm doing that very thing right now. The best way to present a solution to a problem is to first clearly define the problem. Unfortunately, once we do that, we tend to swing the pendulum as far in the opposite direction as possible creating an unbalanced and unending cycle of never finding the truth, which rarely sits in extremes. We create what's known as a logical fallacy—specifically a false dilemma. "You're either for me or against me" paints a very clear picture of an either/or option, but what if the truth is that I don't really care one way or the other about you? We have to be careful not to create situations where we force people to one extreme or another.

If you're not convinced this cycle exists, consider the recent generational cycles in the US. William Strauss and Neil Howe wrote a book, *Generations*[1], on this very subject. The "greatest generation" following World War II was one that espoused the values of hard work, keeping your nose to the grindstone, and was the last generation to insist that their children attend church institutions like Sunday School. We can characterize them as idealists: survivors of the previous war. They strove to create a better world than what they had currently lived through. Their children, the Baby Boomers, eager to get out from under their parents' shadows and heavy-handedness, became extremely reactionary. Their interest lay not in work, but play. Not in war, but love. Not in rules, but freedom. And not in religion. "Imagine there's no heaven. It's easy if you try." Remember? Focus turned from crafting a better society to staying out of others' business. The older generation mandating this new generation carry out values they had long ago rejected did not go over well at all.

The late 70s and 80s came and Generation X became the generation of "more." Gone were the days of peace, love, and happiness. In its stead was the rise of big business, the rat race, and the ruthless climb to the top of the corporate ladder. Economic prosperity grew as this generation did, and now two generations removed from the war, entitlement had replaced hard work. And at the heart of America, everything was about personal improvement and looking out for number one. The 90s came, and with it, a rise in social awareness and civic duty, which replaced the selfishness and internally-driven generation of the 80s. Non-profits exploded in an attempt to help the impoverished and war-torn countries of the world, and the government began to work in the same direction—both militarily and with volunteer programs such as AmeriCorps. Meanwhile, the religious reaction to the "me" generation brought about the Religious Right and the silent majority. Church and politics began to collide in ways that were often beneficial but too often altogether unhealthy. Everyone had their "duty" to perform if they were to be a good "American" or a good "Christian."

All of this led to our current generation. We see the population and government struggling with the "religion in politics" issue. We see the fight between the "go and help the world" crowd and the "leave everyone alone" crowd. And the church finds itself in the crosshairs. It will be interesting to see the results of these conflicts in the coming years, but one thing is certain: Our inability to live in the gray areas will once again force a pendulum swing, and once again keep the system unbalanced for years to come.

The church experiences similar cycles. And in our recent fervor to get people out of the pews and into areas of service, we've made one severe misstep: We forgot who we were serving and what we were building. Now, it was never stated as such. Certainly, very few from the pulpit have ever made the call for more children's ministry volunteers because people need to serve the church. That doesn't go over well. No, we tell people if they want to serve Jesus, they need to serve as greeters. It's the ultimate guilt trip, and it usually works rather well. That, or it drives people away. Either way, it gets people out of the seats, which was our main goal after all, right?

We've been trying. We have been making the attempt to convey how important it was that we build each other up. We've created sermon series' about building the church, complete with construction equipment, hard hats, and cinder blocks, but the message we continue to send is that it's extremely important that we build us a building, even though those were merely visuals to reinforce the point. Unfortunately, that has been lost in translation to our people. If we tell them "we need to build the church," we show them visuals of physical construction, all while announcing that we need helpers and volunteers to make the gatherings run. The one thing that isn't heard? The church is people.

As a church leader, I know this to be true. And yours does too. Deep down, we believe this message is carried on the tips of our tongues and is proclaimed regularly to our people. But it's not. Because even if it's being said on occasion, people tend to hear more with their eyes and their experiences than they do with their ears. Because of this, we need to be extremely intentional about what is said, shown, and displayed not only from the front of the room but also from behind closed doors. The church will always, inevitably, reflect its leadership.

Over a surprisingly short period of time, the faces you put on the stage will show to the congregation not only how to look, but how to dress, how to act, how to communicate, and which catch-phrases are "in." The song choices of the worship leader resonate with a particular subsection. The decision to unpack whole passages of scripture in the sermon rather than having a cornucopia of individual verses to support a point also will attract some and send others packing. What we see, hear, and experience will always tell us what is approved and the things that we do not speak just as loudly as to what we should avoid. The ones who stay look like walking, talking miniature versions of their leaders, and the ones who do not will eventually find a church body where they feel comfortable enough to do that very thing. The church always reflects its leadership. If you're not certain why the congregation does the things that they do, we only have to look at the staff in charge to find our reasons.

I've had friends come up to me in the past and say things like, "Anthony, why is it that <a particular church leader> has no interest in speaking with me and can barely remember my name until it comes time to look for someone to fill in with the kids because someone else didn't show up?" I have no answers, but this speaks loudly to those who are already feeling barely more than a number in a system. Churches with a heavy emphasis on tracking tithing will especially feel the weight of this. Everyone in the congregation *knows* that they're a number—and that number is how much they gave (or didn't give) this month in the offering.

We are so careful in our attempt to make things run smoothly and not "disrupt the worship process" for our congregations that we end up making our means the actual end. Yes, we've got a slick transition, smooth integration, and automated check-ins at digital kiosks. But in return our connection has become shallow, and our actual acts of worship ring hollow because we've forgotten about the actual end goal. That being, creating a space where community can know and be known, and the good news of an ever-loving, ever-forgiving God can offer redemption to even the most *unrefined* and *unpolished* of us.

Are we building an organization? The finely tuned cogs in a precisely designed schematic so that everything happens as planned and we are prepared for any eventuality with accuracy and efficiency? Is this what the bible calls us to do as the body of Christ? More specifically, is this what the bible calls us to do as leaders within that body?

Paul makes it pretty clear in Ephesians 4 what he thought the role of the leaders was to be. The apostles, prophets, evangelists, pastors, and teachers (anyone seemingly in an authority position within the body) had a singular mission. "Their responsibility is to equip God's people to do His work and build up the church, the body of Christ." *(v. 12)*

Equip others to go to work and to build up the body of Christ. Too many of us, however, have taken the shortcut route when reading this verse and instead see *"their responsibility is to build the church."* As a result, our churches have taken on more of an appearance of a Fortune 500 company than a body, which is the metaphor used by Paul in the chapter beyond verse 12.

But, let's be honest. This is not at all the fastest or easiest method. When my kids' room is a mess, I know I have two options: the easy one and the right one. It would be much simpler and faster if I just whipped through the room, gathering stray laundry and replacing books on the shelves. It would be so much less of a hassle. And it would avoid the inevitable struggle that accompanies the other alternative—teaching my girls and encouraging them to clean up after themselves.

"Girls, do you remember now why we clean up as we go? We can avoid taking two hours out of your day dealing with the giant mess you've created for yourself."

"Kalista, it's hard to imagine you're doing much cleaning when I keep finding you sitting in the middle of the floor with a blanket on your head."

"Maleah, I appreciate the fact that you've alphabetized the books that are off the shelf and have now re-read three of them. But they're still not back on the shelf."

"Yes, you have to keep cleaning. And in the 10 minutes you've been continually asking me this, you could have been completely finished."

Hassle. Headache. I want to just do it and be done. So. Much.

Easier. But that's not healthy for them. It doesn't teach them anything other than how to be reliant on others to do their jobs. And it's not healthy for me. I don't need more things to keep control of. I don't think most of us do. The typical human being struggles to let go of areas they control. Even small areas like this are sometimes a big win. And, I need to consistently and consciously be looking for ways to lead my children and help them become leaders themselves. All of that starts with me not doing it all for them.

In His last charge before leaving the earth, Jesus tells us to make disciples (Matthew 28.18-20). This takes an extremely human touch. Systems can't create this for us. It takes intentionality in our interactions, schedule, and the very way that we teach and train as leaders. We have to be building disciples and disciplers, not building an organization.

Dilemma 2: Are We Seeing Church Needs or Seeing Individuals?

The ladies ministry is looking for helpers to coordinate the craft section of their weekly get-togethers. If you have a Pinterest account, we need your help. Chili cook-off is in two weeks. Make sure to sign up in the lobby to bring a pot, and plan to stay after the service. Proceeds go to the youth ministry, and you don't want those kids growing up to become hoodlums because they didn't get to go to Christian-Super-Concert this year. The greeting team has been hit with the flu, and we could really use about four of you to stay for the second service and help hand out bulletins. Church-wide cleanup day is next month. We've included a list of items in the bulletin that we need you to bring, along with a shovel, paint roller, and about 8 hours of your blood, sweat, and tears. It's going to be a great time!

I've spoken to a number of good-hearted, talented churchgoers whose attempts at stepping into the process of building the Kingdom consisted of a public call from a leader, a response by the attendee, a well-intentioned attempt by said person, immense frustration and feelings of failure, and three months later a new public call from leadership because of a lack of commitment from volunteers. What happened? Well, the problem is usually threefold.

First, a public call for volunteers might get you more initial responses but few long-term helpers. Many people will gladly put their name onto a paper, but when you follow up and call them later, there's something else going on that prevents them from following through—because a call to all is a call to none. People want that human touch we've already mentioned. Are you looking for nameless, faceless volunteers to fill a role? You're going to get limited buy-in with an approach like that. Leadership is often looking for commitment from its people to the church but isn't often willing to do the same in return—invest in the people they're asking to invest. This is important, and I don't want you to miss it. Church leaders must be willing to invest in their people if they ever expect the congregation to invest back. But getting to know people and spending time with them creates a much larger relational piggy bank for us to withdraw from. You don't get that from a public call to anyone with a pulse.

Second, you're drawing from a large pool, but that pool is watered down in terms of getting perfect fits for what you're needing. You have a round hole that needs filled, and your call garners square, round, and even triangular pegs. You then utilize time and resources trying to fit each peg into the round hole (sometimes at considerable emotional and relational cost), and at the end of a few months you are usually only left with the round pegs who should have been there in the first place. Sure, some of the others are still around, but their edges have been dulled from being jammed into a place they don't truly fit. Not only will they not be as effective as you'd like, but they also won't be stepping into the areas they're most passionate about or into places where they could truly be an asset as a leader. We're often just happy they're not a liability and our slot has been filled. So you lose a majority of your pool by casting the initial net too wide.

Third, the church goes into the process expecting to make an appeal for volunteers in its ministries every six months or so. There's enough attrition and movement going on that there's a real expectation that a "full" ministry of any sort is going to be working at barely two-thirds capacity in six months if not very well-maintained. And there's frustration as to why people don't follow through with their commitments that seeps into how leadership communicates with the congregation. On the flip side of the coin, the average churchgoer expects to hear these very appeals at least every three months, if not more often, for all the varied ministries of the church. This same churchgoer who has spent any number of years dutifully signing up, burning out, and getting passive-aggressively scolded from the pulpit now only looks at these commitments as temporary guilt-laden assignments rather than life-giving, passionate areas of personal ministry. We feed into our own downward spiral on both sides.

Is there a solution? A different approach to be tried? Or is this an inevitable downside to church ministry? It's been alluded to already that I believe the answer is a relational, individual approach. Where the church has begun to subscribe to a "see a need, fill a need" mindset, I firmly believe we need to start adopting the mentality of "see a person, equip a person."

Let's be honest: Do you think your leaders revel in the idea of having to rebuild, retrain, and regroup a few times a year in order to stay afloat in the various areas of ministry? How much time do you think that takes out of their weeks and months? We all want to leverage our time better. I know from experience that this results in a lot of time daydreaming about what they'd rather be doing with their time as a leader.

If you're anything like me, your own dreams usually revolve around spending more time with individuals. Now, don't get me wrong. Anyone who knows me well knows that I love designing systems. I can build them in my sleep. But the older I get, the more I realize that the systems I'm designing need to cut down on developing and maintaining the machine in order to increase individual discipleship time with people. Even writing this book is an attempt at just that.

It hurts to see things the way they are. So let's step into this brave new world together and see just how deep the rabbit hole goes. Because at the end of the day, I don't want to be known as the guy who made a more efficient status quo. I want to get myself and others refocused on the things of Christ—and he was all about intentionally connecting with individuals.

If we were to do just that—connect with the people around us—what do you think we would find? Are we hitting the felt needs of the congregation? For some, perhaps. For others, we might be tickling the itch just enough to keep them mildly appeased. But for so many others, we may be shocked to learn that the itch we're trying to scratch is in a completely different location than where we're targeting. Awkward.

What if instead of trying to build the perfect ministry for others we leveraged our time to help others step into the ministry that they're individually called to lead? None of these individual ministry opportunities even have to be world-wide game changers. For example, a mom hoping to bless the teachers in her child's public school doesn't need her ideas co-opted by the church and made official. She just needs encouragement that her desires to provide cookies and care packages to the faculty is making a difference. Perhaps also having the occasional like-minded partner pointed in her direction. Likewise, a couple feeling the call to Africa doesn't necessarily need to go through the wringer and be officially brought on as supported church staff in order to be commissioned. But what they certainly do need is lots of contacts, connections, and to be bathed in prayer as they begin their support raising.

It might just be that when we stop trying to create ministries within the church to meet needs, we'll find out what the people's needs are, where their passions are, and how we can better help them all make a forever impact on the Kingdom of Christ. The church is people, remember? A Senior Ministry might not be what you need just because you have a dozen or so in the congregation over the age of 60, especially since you likely have about twice as many new and struggling married couples trying to balance the stress of jobs, newborns, and the transition of living with someone who's so unlike themselves. The Seniors might have a blast pouring into those poor couples with their years of wisdom and experience, and most of the husbands and wives would be desperate for a listening ear and a kind word. But if you create a "Senior Ministry," you're likely to push them toward the "officially recognized ministry," and the more natural outpouring of community might never happen at all. Usually the best solutions are to encourage multi-generational and multi-cultural exchanges, but that's rarely the easy route to take. Instead, we align our demographics and unwittingly allow cliques to form.

Homogenous is rarely a good thing.

Instead, let's promote less our own church-wide agendas and instead celebrate what our people are doing by making a bigger deal about the impact our people are having on the world around them in the name of Jesus. We might just find that "church" we've been trying to build is actually building itself.

Dilemma 3: Are We Telling People What They Should Do or Inviting Them Into What We Are Doing?

The next hurdle we face in this multi-faceted machine is that with lots of people and lots of things to do, we find ourselves with more and more programs, and the need for more and more programs. In many ways, that alone is problematic enough, but programs require people to run them. And, while we experience net gains, what exactly might we be losing along the way?

****

Bob is the senior pastor of a moderately sized but growing church. According to The Barna Group[2], the average protestant church size is 89 adults. 60% of protestant churches have less than 100 adults in attendance. Yes, you read that correctly. Our churches that hover around three or four hundred who still view themselves as a "small church" need to hear this loud and clear. For every one of you, there are a dozen other smaller, struggling congregations—many even in your own communities. For purposes of this exercise, we'll put Bob's church right at the 100 bubble. Let's call the church Promise Church, not only because of the message they preach but because of the promise they show for growth (which is really why we're investigating this fictional entity in the first place, right?).

At this stage in the game, Promise Church mostly functions on the manpower of volunteers. Bob has a part-time secretary that doubles as a receptionist at the facility. The children's director, worship leader, and youth director are all extremely capable free labor, as none of these jobs are deemed more than a few hours a week responsibility. As Promise begins to live up to its name, Bob and the elders decide it's time to bring in an official Worship Leader (with a capital L) that can double as a Youth Pastor. Two part-time positions that, combined, give the church its second full-time position. Promise Church is now at a comfortable 150 in attendance, and they can handle that in the new budget.

The volunteer worship leader tries to settle in as part of "the band" but never really fits in with the new style and eventually drops out from leading in any meaningful way. Meanwhile, the husband and wife who used to lead the youth group were told they were perfect fits to continue "helping" with the group. Unfortunately, their investment in the kids and the emotional capital they had built up is making it hard for the new leader to gain much traction. Between that and a much different approach in leadership, the husband and wife decide it's better to back out gracefully and let the new Youth Pastor have plenty of space to develop the group as he feels led.

Charged into new growth by virtue of a more exciting, dynamic, professional style music presentation at the gatherings and a small surge in middle and high school attendance (along with a handful of their parents), Promise Church sees its best year yet, rising to over 250 in barely 12 months. Along with the increased adults and teens come the younger children in those families, and suddenly Bob and the elders recognize the need to make the children's coordinator a paid position. Since the current leader has been doing such a great job and has developed a rapport with the parents already, they ask her to come on in a part-time role, and she graciously accepts.

Additionally, the part-time secretary/receptionist is now made a full-time employee. With this many new faces and so many people coming into the facility during the week, there's only one person with both the time and knowledge to handle the traffic, so this was a no-brainer in the eyes of the elders.

The year begins to progress, but Bob is beginning to feel the weight of all of those faces—how many of them does he know by name? He can't recall anymore. Many more are also falling through the cracks. There's not a great way for people to get plugged in and feel like they belong in a tight-knit community anymore. Murmurs creep in from time to time about the church getting "too big."

Bob meets with the elders, and they agree that something needs to be done. And so small groups are introduced. It's a way to make the big church small, people are told. You can grow together and become more intimate in settings that are not in the church building. People are all highly encouraged to attend, or even to start one of their own.

This is met with middling success. At 300 people and halfway through the year, the first launch of small groups sees 10 groups started, covering about a third of their Sunday attendance. By the end of the year, now at 350, the groups have dwindled to 7, and there has been little growth in the groups which remain. This means that barely 2 in every 10 people are a part of a small group. Should this be chalked up as a failed experiment?

Bob and the elders say no. With the new year's budget, they hire an associate pastor to head up the small groups and help Bob cover more ground in his individual ministry with the congregation. With a more centralized leader, the groups grow in number to 12, and there's a rise in the every-day congregation attender who gets plugged in thanks to there now being an official champion for the cause. This is a very good thing, and it's evidenced by the growth the church experiences, both personally and numerically. By the end of the year, Promise Church has a regular attendance of 500 and 15 small groups (now all larger than they had been previously). 35% of the Sunday attendance is now involved with a group during the week. That's a big improvement, but not yet up to what Promise's leadership was hoping for.

Bob and the new associate pastor, Allen, begin to press for more details from the other 65% on why they aren't a part of a group. The responses vary, but three big trends begin to develop. One, people want a better way to find a group with whom they share the same demographics, likes and dislikes. Jumping into a new group is too scary otherwise. Two, people are too busy during the week to commit to a consistent schedule. Sundays are the only time they can carve out for something like this. And three, even when they find a group whose schedule fits and the people are marginally tolerable, many are looking for a more defined and consistent curriculum that's been given for everyone to follow. Not knowing what the groups are going to be studying seems to be a problem for some. And some others were even shocked to report that many of the groups they had attended didn't even do a bible study every week! Instead, they chose to have a cook-out on occasion, or invited their neighbors to go bowling after cleaning up the trash along the main thoroughfare. Yes, consistency in curriculum is definitely a must.

Taking all of the responses into account, Promise Church's leadership team devises the following plan for the coming year: Allen would officially become the Groups Pastor. His new role would involve creating (and leading, if necessary) a new Seniors group, a Singles ministry, and a College and Career group. After all, the demographics seem to support that these are necessary steps to continue growing. Allen secretly hoped he could task some of the more assertive members of each of those new ministries to carry the majority of the weight, as the task before him was understandably monumental. He would also be responsible for coming up with an official curriculum to run alongside Bob's messages every week. The best way to maintain structure in the groups would be to make them as homogenous as possible. That way anyone could plug into any group and fit right in.

The church would hire a new executive pastor to tackle the ongoing task of managing the ever-growing list of things happening at the facility and maintaining the organizational structure of Promise Church. There would be expansion in the Human Resources and Accounting side of things as well. The new executive pastor would have his hands full with 6 employees (in addition to himself) and Bob, the senior pastor.

Additionally, it was a guarantee now that Promise Church would be expanding to two services as soon as the new year began. As a result, the split-time Youth Pastor and Worship Leader was given the expanded task of managing two gatherings, and the Children's Coordinator now had two services to handle as well. The Coordinator begins to wonder if she has the ability to hold all this together but insists she'll try her best. The Worship Leader knew this new information would be a hard sell for the current band, and he certainly would need to begin looking for more musicians. His only hope was that he wouldn't lose any of the ones he currently had. The Children's ministry began ramping up requests every week for new children's volunteers—two services meant twice as many leaders needed. And the front door greeters suddenly needed a lot more time and energy than the currently lay leaders could handle alone. A number of classes or groups would begin meeting on Sundays in the extra classrooms during both services, handling the issue of those who had no time during the week. But Promise Church enjoyed the blessing of more growth, so they looked forward to the challenges this second service presented to them.

****

Now, I'll stop there so we can look at what's been happening. Our entirely fictional Promise Church has experienced three years of progress, seeing its total staff expand from two to eight, attendance grow from 100 to 500, and ministries expand from three volunteer positions (children, youth, worship) to seven paid positions (children, youth, worship, groups, singles, seniors, college and career) staffed by three people. It's gone from no small groups to at least 15, with three specialty groups starting soon, and they are going from only one service each week to two. From the usual perspective of church growth metrics, and to the human eye, Promise Church is doing extremely well for itself. But let's look at some of the fallout we may have missed at first glance.

Two entirely capable lay leaders were marginalized as a paid professional came to take their place. While this aided in growth, what we didn't notice was that those leaders never completely plugged into any ministry again at Promise. Perhaps they even left the church eventually. Their avenue for ministry was stripped away from them, and they were told they could help in other ways.

Paid staff requires increased budgets, so while giving continued to increase, Promise began to see their budget belts stretching tighter and tighter as the years progressed. It's the biggest reason why the children's position wasn't already a full-time one, why the Youth Pastor was doubling as the Worship Leader, and why poor Allen was doing the job of at least three or four people. There were going to be more messages about giving in the coming months.

And the decision to go to a second service, while perhaps necessary, put a lot of added stress on the "volunteer base" across the board. Now there were twice as many greeters, twice as many children's workers, extra band members, and every classroom full. There were going to be lots of all-calls to the congregation for help in the coming weeks as well.

Finally, the shift to identical curriculum, while simplifying matters immensely, turned the dedicated leaders of each group into glorified facilitators and hosts. This completely eliminates the opportunity for some with the gift of teaching to properly exercise their giftings, as their new roles would be more administrative and hospitality centered. Additionally, providing a set schedule for groups didn't allow for the missional and community oriented mindset shown by some groups. Now, rather than hosting potlucks, inviting neighbors over for game nights, and doing community clean-up efforts all in conjunction with bible study nights, the groups were all expected to follow a set plan to only have discussion nights and then, only based on the message presented the previous Sunday. As mentioned already, homogenous rarely is healthy, and in this regard, it certainly would not be for Promise Church. This doesn't allow room for the various leaders to assess their groups and speak specifically into their lives with timely words from the whole of scripture. The likelihood for most groups is that the curriculum presented is scratching that non-existent itch again.

I know this was an extremely long-winded way of showing the slippery slope present when we dive into the world of programs and expansions. But I thought it was necessary as it also began to illustrate the problem we're actually addressing: At some point we lose interest in inviting people into what we are doing. Instead, we begin telling them what to do— "sign up for this program;" "join a small group;" "work in the children's ministry." If we aren't careful, the very things that could be beneficial to the congregation turn into mandates accompanied by a guilty conscience if their response is in the negative.

If I were considering building a house, completely of my own accord, I don't think the most effective way to go about it would be to approach my architect and engineer friends saying, "Design me a house, and make it a good one. I need it in two weeks." This would not at all be received well, especially when the news are accompanied by the request that they do it at no charge because "we're friends." And I wouldn't find my general contractor buddy and inform him, "Next month, you're going to build my new house. I've got a handful of other guys I'm going to pull in to help as your workforce. I don't think you should need anything more than money for materials, right?" And I certainly wouldn't start group texting my closest friends demanding that they take vacation time to help me build my new place. Not only would all of that be extremely disrespectful and arrogant of me, but I'd be extremely surprised if I had any friends at all after that. So, why do we insist on taking this approach within the church?

Why do we try to place heavy loads on people and try to pass it off as their "Christian duty"? Jesus promised that His yoke would be easy and His burden light. But I guess many churches didn't get that memo. Or perhaps we did, and like the Pharisees of Jesus's day, we've decided to add to the burden with weights of our own. Paul says that God gives us the perfect example of how to approach this properly:

God will do this, for he is faithful to do what he says, and **he has invited you into partnership with His Son,** Jesus Christ our Lord. I appeal to you, dear brothers and sisters, by the authority of our Lord Jesus Christ, to live in harmony with each other. Let there be no divisions in the church. Rather, be of one mind, united in thought and purpose (1 Corinthians 1.9-10, emphasis mine).

Can we not approach people with the same care and concern that we do outside the church? Is it outside the question for us to know the person we're talking with well enough to simply tell them, "I'm thinking about starting this new project, and I think you would be *fantastic* to partner with." Or perhaps, "Hey, I've been thinking about your strengths and how God has gifted you, and I think you may be just what our team needs. Have you ever considered jumping in and helping out?" It may even be that the person you're speaking to has a better perspective on the ministry you're targeting them for. It could be they're looking for just that right bit of encouragement and empowerment to simply run in the direction they're already wired for.

They may still say no. That's completely allowed, but everyone wants to be a part of something they're invited to—something personal and Intimate. Conversely, no one wants to be told what to do, even if it's what they're generally inclined to do. It grates on us. If we're honest, it's why many of us get into leadership in the first place: When you lead, less people can tell you what to do, right? So why would we come to others with that very same flawed approach?

Do what you are led to do, and allow others to do what they are led to do. Invite. Then participate in the things that others are doing. People will come along because they want to be a part of what is going on. It's called belonging. And in this, there will be harmony. Unity is a beautiful thing.

Dilemma 4: Are We Letting Big Church Inform Everyday Life or Everyday Life Inform Big Church?

Sunday morning has come around again. You're ready, right? The pastor has spent his 20-30 hours of sermon prep time. The band has practiced for a few hours this week, and they're doing another run-through right now just to be safe. Each of them has probably invested at least four to five hours on the service prior to its start time. Your worship pastor, at least double that. The children's ministry is bustling with volunteers—at least two per class plus the free labor we call "helpers" (our own middle school children). Their coordinator likely spent 10 hours of their week just scheduling, emailing, and putting together resources to ensure all of those people are on time and ready to serve. Greeters are at the ready, their third double shot latte in hand and a wide grin on their face (do we really need more greeters than we have swinging double-doors?). The tech team is struggling to figure out the feedback issue with the microphones, test the announcement video, and input the last-minute powerpoint slides for the sermon—all at the same time. By this point, the tech booth has five people trying to do three jobs on two computers.

For any of you who have been on a church staff, you know as frantic as this seems, this is the reality of a Sunday morning. What's more, this is still only the tip of the iceberg when it comes to preparing for what happens on a Sunday. And it barely touches the amount of hands that went into the cookie jar each week in handling the repetitive tasks that we tell ourselves need done. Communion. Chairs. Bulletins. You get the idea. Or, you live there.

And in a flash, it's all over. In an hour, all the hard work and preparation has come to a head, and it's either time to do it all over again (literally in your next gathering), or start planning for next week, where you can do it all over again. Does it ever feel like the Greek King, Sisyphus, forever doomed to push the rock up a hill, but never reaping the rewards of reaching the top and the promised land guaranteed on the other side?

The amount of time invested in putting together a 60 minute presentation borders on the absurd. The amount of manpower to pull it off certainly is far beyond the absurd level, but the big payoff is built to happen on Sunday morning according to the way that today's church works. So it's worth the investment, right?

Let's look at the numbers for a moment. Obviously the specifics will change with every church and every situation, but I hope we can ballpark a few numbers we can all agree on.

First, the paid staff. The teaching pastor (typically also your lead pastor) will likely spend at least 20 hours in sermon prep. Add to that an hour staff meeting every week, mainly devoted to coming Sunday events. Add another hour planning with a creative team to build the weekly liturgy and to ensure elements (music, aesthetics, graphics, etc.) flow together. Factor in another hour or two in meetings to ensure continuity between sermons if you have a multi-site church and there are multiple speakers each week. Even in a highly optimized church setting with quick, to-the-point gathering meetings and a pastor who takes less time than average preparing his sermon, you're still looking at a pastor who spends 20 hours of his 40 hour work week (that's 50% for those keeping score at home) preparing for 1/7th of the week (14.2%). And ask anyone who does public speaking or preaching routinely: They'll tell you that the drain the speaking puts on you is equivalent to at least double the time you took to give the presentation.

Which means that at the end of the week, the typical pastor spends nearly his entire work week either preparing for or presenting at the Sunday gathering. This doesn't provide additional time for vision planning, leadership development, meeting and training ministry leaders, counseling members, handling work emails and returning phone calls, personal prayer and study... you know, little things.

Children's ministry staff will often be one of the first to arrive and last to leave on a Sunday because of the time needed to maintain the sheer volume of volunteers and clean up the inevitable mess of, well, children, everywhere. We'll give them a six-hour Sunday (as all the Children's Directors snicker) and the aforementioned 10 hours of prep time. Add the same staff meeting, and you're looking at at least 17 hours devoted to Sunday. Most churches are only paying the Children's Director part time, which means good luck squeezing in anything else meaningful in the remaining three hours of your week! Try training and developing new leaders, looking at new curriculum, or—God forbid—designing your own, and you're working on your own dime at that point.

Worship leaders will probably have spent at least 12 hours earlier in the week planning, meeting, and practicing with the band. Add to that an early Sunday start and you're looking at anywhere from 3-8 hours on the weekend, depending on the number of gatherings you have.

And we'll stop there, although we all know more staff is definitely used each week. Those three roles alone total 60-80 hours of prep and presentation each week. Some of us have churches where on a good week, we'd be happy to have 60 to 80 people show up. That puts us at a staggering 1:1 ratio of prep and presentation hours per attendee. Obviously, many of you are looking at higher attendance numbers than that, but it still shows the weakness in casting a wide net into a shallow pool hoping for good results. There may be wisdom in considering how you can take even an hour or two out of your week and fish deeper with a more deliberate focus. In those two hours, you could have met for 30 minutes with four of your members in meaningful conversation and development. Multiply that times four weeks, and you could be having a much more impactful, personal ministry with 16 of your members each month than they would ever get from a generic set of sermons developed for average Joe in your congregation during that same month's time.

As an aside, for those of you spending 30+ hours every week just doing sermon preparation, it might be good to cut that back significantly and spend more time with your people. Or maybe, go meet your neighbors. I'm not saying, I'm just saying. Tim Keller, author and pastor of Redeemer Presbyterian Church in New York City, agrees in one interview:

> I would not advise younger ministers to spend so much time [on sermon preparation], however. The main way to become a good preacher is to preach a lot, and to spend tons of time in people work—that is how you grow from becoming not just a Bible commentator but a flesh and blood preacher. When I was a pastor without a large staff I put in 6-8 hours on a sermon.[3]

Reorienting our schedule is one huge way that we can tell people that they're important to us. Failing to do so says that our plans and systems are of more value than the people we claim to be serving. It's no wonder there's often pushback and lack of buy-in from the congregation when they're asked to "give a little bit more" or to volunteer more of their time to the church.

Adding additional gatherings makes things look more efficient—less planning for reaching more people at a time without resetting the planning clock. Ratio of prep time to number of ears who hear the message and spend time worshipping in the building goes way down, and most churches look at this as the next logical step. But what then has to double, triple, and quadruple in number, is volunteers. This is a hard sell.

For example, a church that can handle 400 in the auditorium and 100 children in classrooms operates on anywhere from 25 to 45 volunteers each Sunday service, between children's teachers, greeters, setup and lobby teams, bands, and the audio/visual teams. That's for one gathering. Using the high numbers, that's 11.25% of your adult attendance (not including paid staff) volunteering each week. If the attendance creeps anywhere over 400, we have to roll over into a second gathering. (And that's not considering the fact that once an event hits 85% capacity, statistics show people stop coming back. So realistically, we would have had to deal with this issue much sooner. But, I digress.)

Let's say that this same church has hit 500 adults and 130 children each week. By capacity limits and the precedent already set, we're now looking at needing 50 to 90 volunteers each week. (We'll lay aside the fact that often many of these are the same people, now being *volunteered* to stay 3 hours instead of the previous hour and a half or so.) You're looking at raising an additional 6.75% in your volunteer pool almost overnight (to get to the 18% you would now need). Sure, you might survive until you hit 800 in attendance, but then what? You start the process all over again and need 75 to 135 or more every week just to "keep the doors open."

Is this process doable? Certainly. Is it replicable? Probably. Is it healthy or sustainable? Not likely. Will it be appreciated by the congregation? Not at all. Why? We go back to what was mentioned previously about feeling like cogs in the ever-turning machine, instead of invested, committed members of a family. All of this work. This planning. This preparation. This execution. This manpower drain. All of it is to connect with a thousand or so (or maybe even less!) people for an hour of their time one day a week.

And that doesn't even begin to touch on the monetary weight this forces on the church, and thus, its people. A quick search (and personal, firsthand knowledge) on church budgets compared to their average attendance shows that most churches spend somewhere between $1200-2100 per weekly attendee each year. Put another way, your church has spent at least $1200 on *you* in the last year. The raw numbers might be even more staggering. Churches with an average of 700-800 weekly attendance budget for nearly $1 million each year, while there are churches that I know are averaging in the 15,000 range and have a yearly budget of over $33 million.

Operating expenses cut into a huge chunk of those numbers, and paying personnel is almost always the highest categorical expense a church has. I can't help wondering what else might be done with a million dollars, and it's hard for most of us to wrap our brains around even the concept of 33 million, much less have an idea of what to do with it. Regardless, we can all agree that numbers of this magnitude should go incredibly far in reaching our communities and the world—far more than they do at present.

Unfortunately, at the end of the day or the fiscal year, we have to continue to feed the beast of our own making, and we face an uphill (if not impossible) challenge in turning things around to be anything other than the situation we created. But what if we could? What might it look like to have everyday life inform the way we gather rather than having the gathering dictate everyday life?

I used to be a big proponent of encouraging pastors and leaders to make their gatherings a reflection and celebration of what God was doing in the communities and small groups. It only seemed reasonable that when the body gathered, we should celebrate the wins happening around us that we weren't even aware of. It's encouraging; it's challenging, and it builds up the body. But lately, I've realized that alone falls short if our communities aren't also spending their time celebrating what God is doing in each of our individual lives.

As Christ works within us to say, do, or simply experience incredible things in our everyday lives, we need to have avenues to share those adventures with the people we care about. And I don't mean with a status update on social media and a few "likes." I mean genuine excitement and face-to-face storytelling. On the flipside, when we falter or when we're struggling to see the miracles happening around us, it's our community that pulls us up, turns our eyes back to the empty cross and tomb, and walks with us into a better tomorrow.

If we start here—celebrating each life with the ups and downs that come with it—the inevitable result is that this begins to spill into everything else we do. It's the only way to experience joy the way that James explains it:

> Dear brothers and sisters, when troubles of any kind come your way, consider it an opportunity for great joy. For you know that when your faith is tested, your endurance has a chance to grow. So let it grow, for when your endurance is fully developed, you will be perfect and complete, needing nothing *(James 1.2-4)*.

James says rejoice in trouble. The end result of such an astounding response, due to a tested faith and patient development, is that we will be complete. Such a thing can only happen in community, the place where we can bear each other's' burdens *(Galatians 6.2)*, where we confess our sins to each other *(James 5.16)*, where we forgive one another *(Ephesians 4.32)*, and motivate each other to acts of love and good works *(Hebrews 10.24)*. Community serves to experience true happiness when the needs of others are met *(Luke 10.27)*, to encourage one another and build each other up *(1 Thessalonians 5.11)*, and to know joy in the middle of trials.

All of this happens without the confines of a weekly machine churning. In fact, without the machine, we're more free than ever before to live this out in every area of our lives, at and all times.

Are large gatherings anathema to fulfilling our gospel mission and call to make disciples of all nations? Not necessarily. But I'm beginning to believe that in their current iteration, they just might be. Too much time, energy, money, and other resources are being poured into a gluttonous, bottomless monster bent on growing itself rather than growing the kingdom.

The kingdom is organic. It's planted and it grows. It takes root in places and flourishes. It struggles to hold in other areas. But it spreads. It has to— it's alive. Let's stop trying to build it and simply start watering.

THE ALTERNATIVE

The Alternative

So, is there a way out? Have we created a machine with so many moving parts and having so much circular momentum that there's no way to stop it or even re-route it? And, if there is a light at the end of the tunnel, what is it and how do we get there from here?

We've identified four major dilemmas churches are faced with, but let's revisit them now. First, we've abandoned the call to make disciples who make disciples and have traded it for a desire to build an organization. Second, we've forgotten the primary focus of loving each other by meeting the needs of our fellow believers and made our emphasis about meeting the needs of the church. Third, we spend far more time telling people what they should do than we spend actually doing them together. And finally, we've allowed the triumphs, celebrations, and struggles from our everyday individual lives get overshadowed by the "bigger" impulsive need to gather weekly without using that time to share both our victories and defeats and be built up by our community in the process.

It's a hard, bitter pill to swallow. And I don't claim to have all the answers. I don't even come from a place where I can say I've devised a tested-and-true system that I've used for the past two decades that guarantees immediate success in this area. What I have are stories of broken lives being changed, broken hearts being mended, and broken people coming together in the most extraordinary of ways. Not because a program ran well. Not because a sermon was particularly inspired. Not because the music compelled people to action. But because when homes are made available to hearts that are desperate for love and truth, God does incredible things. As Wayne Cordeiro puts it in "Shrinking the Mega Church," the church should be:

A place to rise and fall, and to rise again without succumbing to failure or ridicule... A place to make mistakes and learn from them rather than being defeated by them. A loving environment that allows learning through error and if willing, to gain lessons that could save from a cataclysmic defeat later on.[4]

When this isn't the environment that's created, when it's hard to see anything but an effort for perfection and production, it puts undue weight on the people who should be flooded with the opposite experience—an experience where they are free to learn, grow, fall down, and get help picking themselves back up.

So, here is what I've learned. There are a lot of arguments (maybe there always have been) about what the church is meant to be known for. There is less debate over why we exist, though even that seems to get cloudy in our vision from time to time. Let us re-establish that before moving on. Jesus gives us the call as His final words before leaving planet Earth:

> Jesus came and told His disciples, "I have been given all authority in heaven and on earth. Therefore, go and make disciples of all the nations, baptizing them in the name of the Father and the Son and the Holy Spirit. Teach these new disciples to obey all the commands I have given you. And be sure of this: I am with you always, even to the end of the age" (Matthew 28.18-20).

Jesus's last words are a beautifully simple and beautifully circular instruction. He says, "With the authority I have, I give you the authority to make disciples, baptize them, and teach them to obey my commands. One of those commands just happens to be... make disciples, baptize them, and teach them to obey my commands." It is in this simplest of statements that we see our sole purpose as a church.

Our bigger arguments come, however, when we get hung up on the "hows" of our purpose. How do we accomplish the task of making disciples? Which method should we use when we baptize? Which instruments are acceptable on stage? How many jokes is the pastor allowed to say in his sermon before he's abusing his station? And how do we get this whole process to replicate beyond our own generation?

Herein is where we run into trouble. Certainly many of us would stand with strong conviction regarding some of these issues, but we should note that all of these concerns, and a myriad of others, are merely secondary. They're what some refer to as state lines. The state of Texas has a considerably different stance on policies than California. Yet, they're part of the same union we call the United States of America. The founding fathers understood this could become problematic, which is why within the defining documents of our nation (particularly the Bill of Rights) we have a Tenth Amendment that reads, "The powers not delegated to the United States by the Constitution, nor prohibited by it to the states, are reserved to the states respectively, or to the people."

Essentially, the decision-making power not given to the federal government in the Constitution should rest on the states or its individuals to determine for themselves. We have a very similar way of looking at the instructions laid out before us in the scripture. Where it is explicitly stated, we draw a hard line in the sand and refuse to cross the line. Every believer should hold fast to those things and be willing to die on those convictions as integral and necessary to our faith. Other things we see as instructive or descriptive, and we build our own little bunkers and hilltops to stand on. These "state lines" should not define us as no longer a part of the same nation. They are merely distinctions which make our denominations or preferences known.

Another perhaps more down-to-earth example of this would be when I tell my two children to clean their room. One of them likes making a list and checking each item off as she completes the task.

Another one likes to start in a particular corner and keep working from edge to edge until it's done. (Now, granted, using the word "like" here should in no way be seen as me implying that my girls actually *enjoy* cleaning their room. Far from it. I mean that there is a preferred method in which they attempt to postpone the inevitable.) I don't really care which method is used, only that they remain within the parameters I set out: They shouldn't get distracted or go into any other room until it's finished, and by all means don't fight about which way is best. Just get it done.

So what are the things which should be our national borders? What are the things explicitly spelled out for us in the Bible that we are to be doing as a church body? And what might be some implicit instructions that go along with those? Here's a few biggies that I see.

The Church Should Be Going

As we've mentioned already, the core command of the church, and indeed the individuals who make up the body of Christ is to go and make disciples of all nations. The very first thing Jesus makes clear to His disciples after reiterating that He has power over all of creation? They need to go in order to accomplish anything. He mentions the same thing earlier in His ministry, and it gives us a little more insight into the way people tick.

Jesus traveled through all the towns and villages of that area, teaching in the synagogues and announcing the Good News about the Kingdom, and He healed every kind of disease and illness. When He saw the crowds, he had compassion on them because they were confused and helpless, like sheep without a shepherd. He said to His disciples, "The harvest is great, but the workers are few. So pray to the Lord who is in charge of the harvest; ask him to send more workers into His fields" (Matthew 9.35-38).

This, we like. This shows Jesus's compassion for people and asks us to pray that God would raise up workers. These were His instructions to them: "The harvest is great, but the workers are few. So pray to the Lord who is in charge of the harvest; ask him to send more workers into His fields. Now go, and remember that I am sending you out as lambs among wolves" (Luke 10.2-3).

Did you catch it? Maybe you did, and your next thought was likely, "Wait, Jesus… you tricked us." Pray that God would raise up workers. And Jesus calmly replies, "Look! You're the answer to your own prayers."

One would think that such an overt instruction wouldn't be forgotten or pushed aside as a secondary afterthought. Unfortunately, too often, it is. Dr. David Platt, author of the book Radical, says the following in his foreword to Francis Chan's Multiply:

> Yet we have subtly and tragically taken this costly command of Christ to go, baptize, and teach all nations and mutated it into a

comfortable call for Christians to come, be baptized, and listen in one location. If you were to ask individual Christians today what it means to make disciples, you would likely get jumbled thoughts, ambiguous answers, and probably even some blank stares. In all our activity as Christians and with all our resources in the church, we are in danger of practically ignoring the commission of Christ.

We view evangelism as a dreaded topic, we reduce discipleship to a canned program, and so many in the church end up sidelined in a spectator mentality that delegates disciple making to pastors and professionals, ministers and missionaries.[3]

We dummy down the responsibility of believers to the point of "bring people and we'll handle the rest." The devastating byproduct of such a simple task is that Christians no longer even know the first thing about *how* to make disciples, even if they wanted to. And so, we don't. We don't go, we don't make disciples, and we don't teach. But our music's pretty good, and our pastor really knows how to stir up a crowd. We leave feeling like the Spirit moved, but if He's moved anywhere, it's out of the building.

A church that isn't going is failing its primary mandate, and despite its best efforts, that's pretty much a guarantee that those churches will accomplish very little in terms of making a lasting impact on the Kingdom of Christ.

The Church Should Be Loving

We could look at a lot of different places here—the greatest commandment of loving God and loving your neighbor, or the even harder instruction to love your enemies. But those are really instructions Jesus gives to the general populous. Is there something more that Jesus says to specifically instruct His followers?

> So now I am giving you a new commandment: Love each other. Just as I have loved you, you should love each other. Your love for one another will prove to the world that you are my disciples (John 13.34-35).

At first glance, this isn't any different from any of the other times Jesus is talking about love, right? So what's the big deal? Well, Jesus indicates here that the disciples' love for each other will be the thing that sets them apart, not their love for their neighbor or their love for their enemies, but their love for each other.

Again, this seems like an easier charge, almost as if Jesus is lowering the bar, but let's just shoot straight here. They say familiarity breeds contempt, that the more intimately you know someone, the more likely they are to really grate on you. And who do you know better than your own family? See, with others, it's easier to show some semblance of love or compassion: Buy a cup of coffee for a stranger, or smile to the person walking down the hall. But we're much more comfortable with family. We're suddenly hit with laziness, apathy, bitterness, comparison, one-upmanship, and cynicism. We know these people as well as we know ourselves, and we know that none of them truly deserve the love we're supposed to show them.

I'm convinced Jesus understood that if we could get a grip on truly showing love to the people in our own body—our own church—that it would spill over into our interactions with people who aren't yet family. But if we love those outside and don't love those inside... Well, there's a word for that: hypocrisy. Suddenly, we don't become an uncommon church; we become exactly what the world expects us to be. "Do as I say, not as I do" hypocrites. The church must love like Jesus. Anything else falls short.

Make no mistake, this isn't a five-year plan. If you struggle with loving your brothers and sisters in Christ, this is a grave issue and should seriously take the matter in prayer before the Father, a trusted Christian mentor, and likely those you struggle with loving. As I've already stated, this is the core indicator to the world of whether you are a true follower of Christ, and we mustn't lay a crooked foundation and expect anything but a crumbling building.

Once we are able to begin loving those within the body, our very family, we can then start to understand how to properly love those without. We do this by showing an unbelieving world the love of Christ for our brothers first, and second, to those we come into contact with. And in this, we should show no partiality. Income level, gender, skin color, nationality, sexual orientation, and yes, even religion. Now, I'm not at all implying that we should embrace practices that are not acceptable in the eyes of a righteous God, but rather that, while the Father may have stated "Jacob have I loved and Esau have I hated," He absolutely gave you and I no such mandate. Love God. Love others. Period.

The Church Should Be Equipping

Look back now at the next part of Matthew 28: "And make disciples of all the nations, baptizing them in the name of the Father and the Son and the Holy Spirit. Teach these new disciples to obey all the commands I have given you."

Jesus uses words like "disciple" (which means student), "teach," "obey," and "commands." It seems like some form of training was expected to be involved. As we've already mentioned, Paul puts it this way in Ephesians 4:11-16

Now these are the gifts Christ gave to the church: the apostles, the prophets, the evangelists, and the pastors and teachers. Their responsibility is to equip God's people to do His work and build up the church, the body of Christ. This will continue until we all come to such unity in our faith and knowledge of God's Son that we will be mature in the Lord, measuring up to the full and complete standard of Christ.

> Then we will no longer be immature like children. We won't be tossed and blown about by every wind of new teaching. We will not be influenced when people try to trick us with lies so clever they sound like the truth. Instead, we will speak the truth in love, growing in every way more and more like Christ, who is the head of His body, the church. He makes the whole body fit together perfectly. As each part does its own special work, it helps the other parts grow, so that the whole body is healthy and growing and full of love.

Using the gifts given to us, it's pretty clear that the mandate is to be "equipping." Why? Equip God's people to do God's work (note, the work wasn't meant to be done by just the leaders), and to facilitate the growth of the body. You've heard the saying, "Give a man a fish, feed him for a day. Teach a man to fish, feed him for a lifetime." The problem with the way most churches are set up is that they're stuck in a constant loop of feeding everyone their fish because nobody knows how to catch their own, and it's creating a generation of believers who will eventually die of starvation if we don't do something about it. We've created a culture where people not only expect to be served and fed. They demand it.

See, we were never meant to live in isolation, but we also weren't meant to grow in isolation. We talk about the need for community all the time. How many people can honestly say that they're being trained— equipped—by someone else in the body? How many can say they're not only being discipled, but they're actively training and equipping someone else? A church steeped in the gospel of Jesus is filled with people who are excited to teach and equip, rather than those who expect someone else to.

Paul has even filled us in on why this matters and the expected outcome. It will bring us to unity. It will make us more mature collectively and individually. We will look more like Christ. We will know truth and recognize false teaching. We will speak not only the truth, but communicate in love. The body will be healthy and growing because each part knows it has an integral part to play and eagerly desires to serve the body in love with its own special work. But it all starts with equipping.

The Church Should Be Encouraging

We find examples of this across both Old and New Testaments, but none more plainly stated than in Romans 1:12 where Paul says, "When we get together, I want to encourage you in your faith, but I also want to be encouraged by yours."

Paul, in fact, makes quite a habit of this all throughout the book of Acts. We see it when he leaves cities, when he returns to cities in which new churches had been planted, and even immediately after being miraculously freed from prison- to encourage the other believers before they left town! He leaves instructions with the church at Thessalonica to continue encouraging one another, which they were apparently doing well. He also gives direct mandates to Timothy and Titus, both young pastors, to make sure they encouraged and strengthened their congregations with good teaching and necessary correction.

Perhaps the most interesting occurrence is in Acts 13:15, where we find Paul attending a Shabbat service at the local synagogue. "After the usual readings from the books of Moses and the prophets, those in charge of the service sent them this message: 'Brothers, if you have any word of encouragement for the people, come and give it.'" This portion of the service we know as the sermon. The Jews would often refer to this as the d'var Torah or the Torah teaching. What I find fascinating here is that the leaders of the synagogue would open the door for others to step forward and build up the people, not with words of instruction or a how-to list to improve your life, but with words which both encourage and strengthen. Jesus, recognized as a gifted teacher, is invited on at least one occasion to do the same thing in the gospel of Luke.

Encouragement. It's one thing to provide the tools and instruction necessary to perform a task. It's another thing entirely to be built up and strengthened to the point of actually believing you can succeed at said task. Both are extremely vital. We identify gifts in one another and we strengthen and build each person up as they utilize and put into practice the unique giftings they have received.

The Church Should Be Empowering

Just as it is not enough to merely teach and instruct each other, so too it is not quite sufficient to simply equip and encourage. Most of the time, these two need to be accompanied by a public acknowledgement that individuals not only have the tools they need to set out on their journey, but they also have open support from their family and leadership. I have seen far too many situations occur within the church where an individual was given the "go-ahead" to run with a particular idea or task, only to have it fail miserably. Inevitably, one of the things muttered by the one who was left to fall flat was that they felt like they didn't have the support and backing of the upper leadership. Not surprisingly, the same upper leadership responds by saying they felt they gave ample authority and free reign on the project and were surprised to see things not come together.

The issue? A private acknowledgment of authority carries no weight. My children know this. "Daddy said it was my turn to play!" holds no true power when blurted out by my six-year-old to her sister, two years her elder. But you know what does? A booming "Kalista! Listen to your sister!" from across the house.

Our co-workers know this. If you approach those you share an office with and suggest that the boss put you in charge of the new project, those in the room would rightly scoff and ignore you offhand. But if they all received a simple email memo stating exactly the same thing, or even better, if the boss himself popped in to get everyone on the same page, suddenly you have a team snapping to attention. Well, maybe that's a bit much. But they're likely at least a good bit more cooperative, right?

Unfortunately, we must have missed said memo when it comes to empowering people within the church. I believe that this one failure alone may have neutered more disciples of Jesus attempting to make an impact for the Kingdom than any other singular misstep by the church in history.

"I dreamed of changing the world, but my dream didn't even make it to launch. I felt alone and without any support system, so I gave up entirely." I bet you can relate to this on some level. I know I can. It's a tale too often told within the church community. Lack of support and failure to recognize those in our midst who have been gifted to make a splash for the Kingdom of God have stymied far too many of us and will continue to do so.

How much greater would our collaborative impact be on the world if our approach was one of publicly passing on authority and empowering others to do great things? We must take the example of Moses and Joshua in Numbers 27:

> So the Lord said to Moses, 'Take Joshua son of Nun, a man in whom is the spirit of leadership, and lay your hand on him. Have him stand before Eleazar the priest and the entire assembly and commission him in their presence. Give him some of your authority so the whole Israelite community will obey him. He is to stand before Eleazar the priest, who will obtain decisions for him by inquiring of the Urim before the Lord. At His command he and the entire community of the Israelites will go out, and at His command they will come in.' (vv. 18-21 NIV)

God tells Moses to promote essentially his administrative assistant (and part-time army general) in the presence of all the people. The high priest would verify that the appointment was from God, and Moses would command everyone to obey Joshua. This is important, as Moses showed up on the scene completely on his own. Sure, he had the backing of a handful of plagues to bolster his claim, but there was no one standing before the Israelites proclaiming Moses as leader. However, with a commissioning like this, the response of the people to Joshua's first official command was as follows:

> They answered Joshua, 'We will do whatever you command us, and we will go wherever you send us. We will obey you just as we obeyed Moses. And may the Lord your God be with you as he

was with Moses. Anyone who rebels against your orders and does not obey your words and everything you command will be put to death. So be strong and courageous!' (Joshua 1:16-18)

It's important to note that this is a great deal different from the people's typical reaction to Moses. Contrary to what they hint at here, the Israelites weren't all that great at obeying Moses. It seems on more than one occasion, their reaction was more akin to "who put you in charge?" But with Joshua's public empowerment and commissioning, nothing was left in doubt. He carried the authority he claimed to have. It's a powerful lesson we should all take to heart.

THE ALTERNATIVE

The Church Should Be Confessing

While it should be noted in James 5:16 that we are called to confess our sins to one another, not just before God alone (and boy, do churches need to do a better job of admitting when we screw up), there's a final area that Jesus himself says would be the foundation of His church. You can be doing all of the things mentioned previously, but without this singular area, you are not a biblical church.

> Now when Jesus came into the district of Caesarea Philippi, he asked His disciples, "Who do people say that the Son of Man is?" And they said, "Some say John the Baptist, others say Elijah, and others Jeremiah or one of the prophets." He said to them, "But who do you say that I am?" Simon Peter replied, "You are the Christ, the Son of the living God." And Jesus answered him, "Blessed are you, Simon Bar-Jonah! For flesh and blood has not revealed this to you, but my Father who is in heaven. And I tell you, you are Peter, and on this rock I will build my church, and the gates of hell shall not prevail against it (Matthew 16.13-18 ESV).

Jesus says that the foundation on which he would build His church is the confession that Jesus is "the Christ, the Son of the Living God." This is extremely significant. It is, in fact, the pinnacle of which the entirety of the gospel hangs. The apostle John is explicit in His statements about this in his first letter.

> So I am writing to you not because you don't know the truth but because you know the difference between truth and lies. And who is a liar? Anyone who says that Jesus is not the Christ. Anyone who denies the Father and the Son is an antichrist. Anyone who denies the Son doesn't have the Father, either. But anyone who acknowledges the Son has the Father also (1 John 2:21-23).

You cannot have the Father without the Son, and on this, we deviate from all of the other monotheistic religions that the world claims are related. Christians, Jews, and Muslims will never agree on the answer to the question "who is Jesus?" But as Christians, the thing we hold to as most important is that Jesus is exactly who He claimed to be. Without this pronunciation, we merely practice a set of moral ideals loosely following a rebellious prophet or a strict code of religious laws with no hope of salvation from ourselves. The name Jesus Christ *must* be on the tips of our tongues when we interact with others. He is the only path to salvation and He is the only hope for redemption. Paul says it this way in Romans 10:9: "If you openly declare that Jesus is Lord and believe in your heart that God raised him from the dead, you will be saved."

Confessing—Jesus is the Christ, the Son of the Living God. We will talk about the manger in months other than December. We will talk about the cross even if it's uncomfortable. We will boldly proclaim His perfection, His deity, and His resurrection. We will unashamedly look forward to His return, because Jesus is the focus of our church. Jesus is the reason for our church. It's all about him. It's all for him.

The Church Should Be A Body

"The human body has many parts, but the many parts make up one whole body. So it is with the body of Christ" (1 Corinthians 12:12).

Paul begins one of his most familiar metaphors for the church with this simple statement, and it's loaded with meaning. He continues, "Yes, the body has many different parts, not just one part" (v 14).

If you're anything like me, you've spent considerable time pondering the importance of this verse and wondered just when those other parts might have a chance to be of use. Even if you haven't, I'm willing to bet that you've at least had the more personal thought of "What good am I?" run through your mind at least once.

We all have heard that everyone is given particular gifts. We're all told that every individual is important. We hear that it's important to find out where we best fit and then are encouraged to plug in and give it our all! But what we hear and what we see may not often line up.

We take a look up on the stage and see charismatic, talented individuals passionately leading worship. We see devoted, well-spoken communicators conveying a timely truth about the gospel or rallying the believers to action. We look around the lobby and find outgoing, friendly faces willing to offer a smile, a firm handshake, and directions to the nearest restroom. And we see classrooms full of cheerful teachers, eager to tackle the responsibilities of caring for and instructing our children. As a result, while we're told that we're all individually important, what we see is that we don't fit one of those moulds. Then, the wheels start spinning in our own minds. Maybe we're doing it wrong. Maybe we should try to be one of those people we see every Sunday. Maybe we're a failure. Maybe *God* is the failure. The downward spiral goes ever on if we allow it.

This is allowed to continue in our churches. Certainly, I don't believe it's out of any malicious intent at all. In fact, if presented with the case, I would imagine every single church would adamantly decry the idea entirely. We know this isn't the way to go about things, and we know it's not at all healthy. Paul even tells us so as he continues his thought in 1 Corinthians 12.

> If the foot says, 'I am not a part of the body because I am not a hand,' that does not make it any less a part of the body. And if the ear says, 'I am not part of the body because I am not an eye,' would that make it any less a part of the body? If the whole body were an eye, how would you hear? Or if your whole body were an ear, how would you smell anything? But our bodies have many parts, and God has put each part just where he wants it. How strange a body would be if it had only one part! Yes, there are many parts, but only one body. The eye can never say to the hand, 'I don't need you.' The head can't say to the feet, 'I don't need you' (vv 15-21).

The truth is we do need each other. We need *every* part to do its part. When people are missing from our gatherings (large or small), we should feel it. Remember, Paul tells us in Ephesians 4 that the body is only healthy and growing if each part is doing its own special work. This seems to imply pretty clearly that when there are parts that aren't doing their work or missing entirely, the body suffers and doesn't grow. Paul continues in 1 Corinthians 12:

> In fact, some parts of the body that seem weakest and least important are actually the most necessary. And the parts we regard as less honorable are those we clothe with the greatest care. So we carefully protect those parts that should not be seen, while the more honorable parts do not require this special care. So God has put the body together such that extra honor and care are given to those parts that have less dignity. This makes for harmony among

the members, so that all the members care for each other. If one part suffers, all the parts suffer with it, and if one part is honored, all the parts are glad. All of you together are Christ's body, and each of you is a part of it (1 Corinthians 12:22-27).

Imagine a football team that only trots out 10 players onto the field, or a potluck where the person bringing the plates forgets to show up. We feel it. We do our best to make it work, but we know there's something missing because everyone else has to do some extra work to make up for the deficit.

Our gatherings should feel the same way. If the pastor doesn't show up to preach, everyone notices and cares, but what about the woman who sits alone in the row in front of you? Is her absence as noticeable? What special work does she bring to the body that is no longer present when the church gathers? Do you even know? Does the church leadership?

All of us are Christ's body. Not alone, but together, in unity. Note that Christ is the one in charge. Be wary of any church who blindly follows its pastor. The church should be a full body with Christ as the head and no man. It should work as one, with every part doing its part. In the next chapter, we will dive deeper into how this might look in our gatherings.

The Church Should Be A Family

The last idea I want us to consider is that we should look a lot more like a family than a business. I know, the current trend is to run our churches with slick marketing campaigns, trendy social media, a CEO-styled senior pastor with a COO for an executive pastor, and a business-modeled staff hierarchy in order to achieve mega-church status. But I think this fails us, and probably the Kingdom, on many fronts.

In our family, my wife is happy to have a full-time job as an architect. I split my time in many directions- as a writer, entrepreneur, business consultant, personal development coach, music instructor, father of two, dishwasher, grocery shopper, cook, chief floor cleaner, and the list goes on. We know our roles and what is typically expected of us. We do our best to chip in and help each other as much as possible to make things work as smoothly as a family of four could.

My girls do their best (most of the time) to help as well. They know they need to keep their bedroom and toy room clean, though this usually takes designated times each week in order for them to actually act on what they know. The oldest is in charge of taking out the recycling and putting the cold groceries away. The youngest dumps the little trash cans all around the house and handles pantry items when we return from shopping. Both are expected to help set the table for dinner. They know this and, for the most part, are happy to participate.

Well, no, that's not exactly true. My oldest, who is 8, is notorious for doing anything she can possibly think of to get out of doing work. If I ask her to help me with something around the house, she suddenly develops the irresistible urge to use the restroom, where she then proceeds to hide out for as long as she possibly can in hopes of my forgetting the request. If I insist on her helping, she usually starts the task, works for a total of two minutes, and then flops on the couch with a book in her hand to begin reading.

"Kalista, I don't think you're done with what I asked you to do."

"But it's not fair!"

"What's not fair?"

Lips pursed, eyebrows furrowed, she continues. "Why do I have to do everything?"

"Um, Kalista, you don't have to do everything. In fact, you don't have to do most things."

She's realized after a few years of this routine that if she pushes down this road too far, my response is to list the litany of things that I, in fact, do for her. I then threaten to stop doing said things if she can't acquiesce to my simple request to just move her backpack somewhere other than the doorway it's currently residing in. Her new tactic is to clarify her previous statement.

"I mean, why do I have to do everything that has to do with my stuff?"

Fish in a barrel, folks.

But, while my 8-year-old may not have developed the best debate skills yet, the principles underlying family responsibility are currently being reinforced daily with both her and her sister. It may not always work as smoothly as it should, but hey, that's the idea with family, isn't it?

Together we work on developing organizational skills, priorities, and learning responsibility. We begin to instruct our children on what it means to participate in a family unit. They start to understand that things are better when we work together and are also more fun when done in community. Through cooking, we teach them basic math and measurements, but they also learn the value of teamwork and the positive results of hard work. When working on homework and projects, they get insights into how to better approach issues and learn problem-solving techniques, but they also get a chance to talk about their day and how they got into a fight with their friend.

Sometimes there are breakdowns in communication. Sometimes my kids don't want to obey, even when they know they should.

Sometimes my wife loses her cool with them. Sometimes I raise my voice. Sometimes we do things that we have to go back and apologize for later.

But that's the beauty of being a family. We allow for mistakes. We grow together through the good times and the bad, and we are around for each other 24/7. The business model we too often adopt falls short of this because it's results-driven instead of relationship-driven. It focuses on achievement rather than growth and hierarchy rather than togetherness.

The church should be a family. One that is intimately and intricately involved in each others' lives all week long with all the joy, sorrow, and mess that comes with it. There is no "success" involved when you're called to a friend's house at midnight and end up having to Baker Act them in an effort to save them from themselves. But there is family. There are no "results" when a young soon-to-be mother calls you at 3am asking for a ride from across the state because she doesn't know where else to go, and she made a mistake in leaving home. But there is love and compassion. There are hard lessons to learn and forgiveness to be offered. There are long hours with the lights on at night working through family trouble, parenting issues, drug addiction, and a whole litany of other messes that the organized church doesn't want to begin to touch. It's too messy. It doesn't preach. And it certainly doesn't produce growth and results. But hardship does bring families together. So, don't be afraid to jump in and get messy. It's ok. Then you'll be certain there's already someone in the mess with you when you're the one needing to be dug out.

THE DREAM

We've talked about the dilemmas and issues arising from a church model that is focused on self-maintenance. We've also looked at a few key parts of scripture to determine a number of things that the church *should* be. Knowing those things, it's still not exactly wise to attempt to prescribe a hard and fast solution for all churches everywhere. We don't want to create a checklist where people can turn this into yet another achievement-based system. There are too many of those already. What we can do though, is dream. In my mind, vision creates direction, which is a necessary eventual step, but dreams offer a promise of hope.

And so, just for a moment, dream with me. Not of a personal preference where all our desires are fulfilled, but of a place where the gospel is preached, a place where mercy and justice collide in a perfect example of the jealous love of God, and His desires are the driving force for our decisions instead of our own. If we were speaking face to face, this would be the point where I would ask you to close your eyes, but that would make your attempts at reading much more difficult. So instead, open your mind and your heart. See if the dream doesn't warm and inspire you to desire more than the mundane.

We dream of a gathering that is authentic. Personally authentic because we long to live our lives without fear of judgment and without wearing masks in order to "fake it" with those around us. In this dream, we openly admit mistakes and confess failures and doubts because this is a place of transparency and openness—both to confess brokenness and to receive those who are broken. Structurally authentic, the gathering contains nothing put-on, forced, out of place, or overly produced. This does not mean lacking in innovation or creativity, but it does mean we are aware of who we are and who we are called to be. We don't try to live individually or corporately as something that we are not.

We dream of a space that is interrupted and interruptible. Jesus lived an interrupted life and he put himself into positions which forced him to be interrupted. We want to have spaces where both are also true. If something is said or done that requires further clarification or raises questions or doubts, we dream of a place that welcomes and embraces hands going up, questions being asked, and rehearsed messages going by the wayside in order to better facilitate the growth of those present. To further encourage this, we want to create environments where open conversation and discussion are the norm, and the focus of our attention is less on a figure at the front of the room, more on the people around us, and mostly on Christ.

We dream of a place filled with expressions of love, joy, peace, patience, kindness, goodness, gentleness, and self-control. Expressed by all, confessed to all. The fruit of the Spirit, Paul tells us in Galatians 5, are the characteristics portrayed by all who have the Holy Spirit indwelling them. If that is the case, shouldn't this be even more readily apparent and expressed within our gatherings? And in the days that I am lacking in patience, my fellow brothers and sisters build me up, encourage me, and yes, correct me. In the times that I see expressions of gentleness and kindness conveyed to others, I should encourage that behavior to continue. What better way to build up the body of Christ than make a focal point of our gathering to be exactly that?

And so, **we dream of a place where the work of Jesus in individual lives is celebrated corporately.** There is no greater way to build up and encourage the body than to celebrate the work of Christ, our head, doing incredible things through us, the parts of the body. And as we grow and are knit together in unity, we grow in maturity, and come to the fullness of maturity that we saw Paul speaking of in Ephesians 4.

We dream of a space where the assembled body can work together, each using their unique giftings to accomplish something more powerful, more spirit-filled, and more amazing than anything we could accomplish alone. This is not a place to come, sit, face a wall, hear some words, and leave feeling empty as only a handful among us have used our gifts to the fullness. In the medical sense, a body with those characteristics would rightly be considered a vegetable or at best, one with extremely atrophied muscles.

We long for gatherings that openly require the gifts of everyone present. When I walk through the door and need a word of encouragement, there are those present who are available. If someone needs prayer for healing or wisdom spoken to them about a tough situation, we have people ready and willing to exercise their gifts to benefit the body in these ways as well. We dream of a place where teaching and counsel is shared with wisdom by many who have received the gifts, and not just a singular voice. If each member is as important as we are told, each member should have adequate space to exercise the gifts they've been given.

It's no wonder that the majority of our congregations don't have the first clue about how to put their gifts into practice. We don't allow them the space or opportunity in which to use them. The result is that these body parts stop functioning. Instead, **we dream of the gathering being the first and easiest place to practice our gifts before being thrown to the wolves in the world**. This gives us the confidence that He who called us is faithful, and He will not leave us. We will feel better prepared and more comfortable in our own skin and with our own voices.

We dream of a place where the truth of the gospel is interwoven in every expression of every believer we come in contact with. A place where we stop with the platitudes and self-help and instead fix our eyes on Jesus, the Author and Perfecter of our faith.

We dream of creating an environment where we are meeting individually and in groups throughout the week, not because we are obligated to, but because we feel compelled to. We love our fellow believers enough that we are fully and deeply invested in each other's personal lives. We long to bring others into this fellowship and community, not because we want to invite them to church, but because we want them to experience the truth of who Jesus Christ is in a real and personal way. And we know that the best way to lead them into this is through relational connection and not a generic invitation.

We dream of a way for our lives to inform our groups and for our groups to inform our gatherings, not the other way around. The joys and frustrations we are experiencing are fully addressed in any space in which we gather because we are open and transparent, and we know that the best way to build up and equip the church is to provide timely, individualized training rather than one-size-fits-none expressions.

In short, **we dream of a place where nothing happens within that doesn't already occur in some form during the week.** There is little that should be attempted in any way that the body cannot already be expressing individually in the places where we live, work, and play. If we have built a formula where any number of things we believe to be "Christianity" cannot be readily lived out in our daily lives, we have a formula that is unhealthy.

And **we dream of a community in which giving to others is exercised in four different and important ways.** First, we dream of an environment where the focus should be giving first to those in need within the body. This may be monetary, and likely will be. "If someone has enough money to live well and sees a brother or sister in need but shows no compassion—how can God's love be in that person? Dear children, let's not merely say that we love each other; let us show the truth by our actions" (1 John 3:17-18). Then we give to provide for or supplement leaders as needed. It likely won't require a full complement of full-time church staff to make this work anymore. Perhaps it's time for more of us to become "tentmakers" in our own right. But, when the need arises, we provide for those that God has given us to lead and direct the church. Next, we give to those in need within the international body. This is not a secondary mandate, but a primary focal point. We go, we give to those who are going, and we give to those in every part of the world who has need because they are fellow brothers and sisters and it is our calling. And finally, we give to impact the Kingdom God is building locally. Not to support programs, but to build the Kingdom. This is not our main focus, and if our budget is created in a way that building maintenance, mortgages, and local ministries take up the bulk of our giving, we dream of a church willing to rethink the way that money is used to better reflect the mission of the church, even if it means letting go of our own little kingdoms along the way.

This is not an exhaustive list meant to root out any and all areas of emphasis that don't fall into these categories, but it's a starting point. This is not a checklist in order to determine how spiritually strong or deficient our church is. This is an idea, and ideas are very dangerous things. Ideas can topple empires, end centuries of injustice, or completely reshape the way we look at the universe itself. But I believe if we continue down this road—if we allow ourselves moments of divine discontent for the purpose of doing all things with excellence to the glory of God—I believe that deconstructing church is exactly the place where we need to begin. Where we end up? I suppose that's up to you. I suppose that's up to us.

Appendix

1. Strauss, William, and Neil Howe. *Generations: The History of America's Future, 1584-2069*. New York: Morrow, 1991. Print.

2. "Small Churches Struggle to Grow Because Of The People They Attract." *Barna Group*. 02 Sept. 2003. Web. 26 Jan. 2016.

3. Adams, Colin. "Tim Keller Answers 10 Preaching Questions." *ChurchLeaders.com*. 2012. Web. 26 Jan. 2016

4. Cordeiro, Wayne. *Shrinking the Megachurch*. Exponential Resources, 2003. EBook.

5. Chan, Francis, Mark Beuving, and David Platt. *Multiply: Disciples Making Disciples*. CO Springs, CO: David C Cook, 2012. Print.

ABOUT THE AUTHOR

Anthony Anderson lives in Orlando, FL with his wife and two daughters. He is a member of Catalyst Coach (catalystcoach.org) and dedicates his time toward leadership development. His personal why is "Sheep to Shepherds" and strives to make every effort to work that out in his day-to-day life. He leads various small groups and is available for organizational and individual coaching, as well as speaking engagements at churches, businesses, and conferences. He sometimes maintains a blog at www.despisedsamaritan.com .

Printed in Great Britain
by Amazon